My growing and running a successful Business

INDUX

Step #1:**Why Your Business Growth May Become Stagnant**

Step #2:My up to date updated recommendations For growing and running website.

Step #3: GDPR is putting an end to that!

Step #4: Powers like that get my attention!

Step #5:**Adding a Personal Touch to Your Brand Through Influencer Marketing**

Step #6: **A Halt in Traffic: Lack of Reviews is Effecting Your Business and Here's Why**

Step #7:**Why Your Mailing List Is Your Most Powerful Online Marketing Tool**

Step #8:**The Benefits of Email Marketing**

Step #9:**Why You Need To Get Into The Mind Of Your Audience**

Step #10: **How To Use Targeted Ads To Generate Traffic With Facebook**.

Step #1:Why Your Business Growth May Become Stagnant

Strategies for lead generation and internet marketing are constantly evolving. You might have been trying certain strategies which have been touted as effective for driving traffic to your online business, but find that they're not working as well for you as others claim they do for them. Your online sales have a significant impact on the growth of your business so you'll need to analyze your current strategies to see what may be going wrong.

The information to follow looks at things you might be doing which are working counter to the growth of your business. Really taking a good look at them will help you to shed these unproductive habits and develop a fresh approach to the online marketing of your business.

You've Not Created An Audience
The most effective way to generate traffic to your online business is to have a strong personal presence. You can accomplish that by authoring articles for authority websites, guest posting and having podcast interviews conducted with you. Doing this presents you as an expert in your field and will certainly get you a following.

You're Not Focused On Establishing Connections
With that being said, you'll need to strike a balance so that you don't present yourself to your audience as an aloof expert. Let them see you as a person with whom they can truly connect and this'll do wonders for your business.

You're Too Dependent On Social Media for Marketing
Social media provides a free platform for you to be able to reach the global market and direct attention to your business. To be most effective if you choose to use social media as a marketing tool, you'll need to make use of the paid ads they offer to get the greatest opportunity. Outside of that, you'll also have to use the services of other forms of paid advertizing outside of social media if you want to see tangible results.

Your Brand Is Not Original
While an important way to get yourself noticed and become profitable is to take a lesson from successful businesses, you'll need to exercise caution not to become a carbon copy and lose your unique identity. There's also no guarantee that you'll have the same success using someone else's strategies. Your best bet is to establish your brand as an original and use that to generate interest in your business which will convert into profitable leads.

You Need To Update Your Marketing Tactics
With the evolution of online marketing strategies, you'll also want to take a close look at your methods to make sure they're current and effective. The online marketing landscape changes so quickly these days, that what may have worked so well for you just a few months ago, doesn't have the same efficacy now. Keep up to date with current strategies by doing research on reputable (authority) sites, to see how you can implement the fresh strategies and put them to work for you.

The competition in the internet market place is quite fierce, but there's always room for more. To make a meaningful impact you have to be willing to do what it takes to set your business apart so that you'll get noticed and attract the right kind of traffic, the profitable kind. You also have to be mindful that there's a lot of information out there clamoring for your attention, begging for you to implement strategies and tactics that are proposed to help you.

Giving serious attention to the foregoing setbacks which may be affecting your business, and having a clear vision in mind as to where you want your business to go, will help you to see renewed and sustained growth.

Step #2:My up to date updated recommendations For growing and running website.

1. Your internet site ought updated load fast. (up to date Google and up to datemersupdated like it!) watch out for reminiscence intensive plugins or conflicting plugins etc. right here are sixteen methods up to date boom internet site speed.

2. safety from hackers is vital, you may want their help. up to date the fact we introduced Sucuri website protection updated our internet site over 2 years ago, we haven't had any problems. I highly suggest which you get it.

3. continually use a .com and except there sincerely is no opportunity don't use a sprint / Hyphen in between phrases in a site name.

4. construct an e-mail listing from day one. go get Popup Domination.

5. web sites do destroy! Some times for up to date up-to-date no cause, pages will forestall showing as they up-to-date or even links gets up-to-date. This often is due up updated a struggle with one of the plugins we use. up-to-date inner and external links up-to-date damaged, I propose you use damaged link Checker.

6. facebook, Twitter & Pinterest. select one and dominate it, up-to-date sucking in any respect 3. Or alternatively, lease a person up-to-date appearance after your social media and cause them to account for the final results.

7. Have a plan up to date enterprise (internet site) – I imply bricks and mortar enterprise without a business plan is quite stupid! Why need up updated it's any distinctive for your website? Have a plan for the coming month, three months, 6 months, 12 months! wherein do you notice you and your internet site five years from now? Do you have got a go out plan? Do you have a sales plan?

"through failing updated up-to-date, you are getting ready up-to-date fail."

eight. if you cognizance on one up-to-date source, you are lacking out. Google, Social Media, email advertising, Podcasts, films, associates, InfoGraphics & Linkbait are all crucial.

9. Consistency is prime when publishing content material. daily, Weekly, up to date, you select how frequently updated publish and up to date updated it. (Gee, I am not usually amazing at following this Rule myself – but definitely, it is crucial!)

"It's now not what we do once in a while that shapes our lives. It's what we do continuously."

10. Make it easy for human beings updated touch you. what's extra, be open up-to-date some criticism or less than tremendous remarks about your internet site. positive a few feedback will come from typically terrible human beings however my usual enjoy is that people want updated assist. for instance, I have obtained a hundred's of emails from human beings notifying me of bugs and spelling mistakes.

eleven. The early fowl trap's the trojan horse, a pronouncing you're possibly heard frequently earlier than. Take as an example a person who bought enterprise.com in 1997 up to date updated up-to-date sell it for $7.five million 2 years later. ok, possibly you can't do this normal however don't think this is a remoted case, opportunities are all around us. Take as an instance Twitter.com – the first few marketers who got on it have been up-to-date take advantage of it earlier than new guidelines got here up-to-date place up to date slow you down from adding humans. when you see possibilities, take it!

12. by no means retaliate up-to-date feedback or emails. human beings will disagree with you and you might even suppose they're dumb, but they're entitled up to date their opinion. Frankly, we don't have the time or strength updated show them incorrect. It's also now not so crucial which you want up to date waste your existence up-to-date prove your self-right and someone else wrong.

this is one among my father's favorite costs – now not every person gets it the first time, but think about it!

"Do you need to be updated be proper or do you want up to date be satisfied"

thirteen. Ask! you can get plenty up-to-date by way of simply asking. whilst up-to-date 18, I stuck Glandular Fever in Ghana and spent an awful week in sanaupupdated in Ghana earlier than returning up-to-date England and spending every week in health center right here inside the united kingdom. I up-to-date relaxation for months after that and decided I had not anything higher up-to-date do then ask people updated do interviews for Retireat21. I spent days emailing hundreds of updated net marketers for interviews. three of the up-to-date one hundred websites in the world came again up to date me and stated they might do an interview, plus over 50 different successful CEOs and marketers.

14. frequently ask your self – If in 10 years (or in sooner or later, 6 months. I yr, five years) you have been up-to-date appearance lower back at your actions up to date day what would you have got changed? try this. From my appropriate friend Craig Ballantyne

15. these days there's an increasing fashion that the people who make the most cash online, purchase a high percent in their up-to-date (pay for commercials). basically, they have got learned additional abilities up-to-date on lead technology and price in keeping with Acquisition (CPA). in case you aren't adding up to date these competencies, you're lacking out. I now include offered traffic in my online promotions.

sixteen. up to date list articles nonetheless bring me 80% of my visiupupdated, even though it most effective up to date on 20% of my time up-to-date create them.

17. In my revel in, it's easier up-to-date a day productively then give up updated it productively. (nicely... up to date now up to date nowadays I've executed not anything, I wager I'm able up updated strive up-to-date the following day updated..)

18. Don't put all of your eggs in a single basket – especially with the way you monetize your internet site.

So regularly, humans have simplest one or two methods of monetizing an internet site up-to-date banner advertising and marketing. however, advertisers come and move and no month is ever the same. Diversify your profits with one of a kind techniques such as affiliate advertising, electronic mail advertising, and marketing, training, ebooks etc! And with associate marketing, promote multiple offers.

additionally, don't presume what you're doing right now, might be working in up to date come. maintain innovating & educating.

nothing is for sure in existence or enterprise, just due up updated something has worked up updated, it doesn't suggest up-to-date work once more up-to-date. this applies up-to-date marketing, promoting, up to dates updated, advertisers. There without a doubt are no guarantees – the handiest assure you could depend on when it all comes up-to-date it, is your self!

19. surround yourself with successful human beings. Retireat21, IncomeDiary & PopUp Domination all came from 'striking out' with other well-matched people.

20. always have a written and signed settlement up-to-date partners / Joint Ventures. people will rip you off for much less cash then you definitely could imagine. Greed is loopy up to date. study: eleven crucial lessons From Going In up-to-date commercial enterprise With human beings

21. What you cognizance on is what you get – so in case you need cash, cognizance on it! always be aware of who owes you money, take a look at that the payments you assume up-to-date receive are arriving on your financial institution account (Paypal account) at the suitable time. if you still receive a commission through a cheque – bank it right now and don't go away it putting around for days.

22. Don't be fearful of the particularly aggressive area of interest! The cause they are aggressive is up-to-date there may be cash in that area of interest!

23. when negotiating, frequently it's far extra powerful up to date updated not anything. I locate that people don't like silence and could need up-to-date something, frequently lowering the charge.

24. preserve transferring ahead. Don't surrender – the biggest difference between fulfillment and failure isn't always giving up.

"Our greatest weak spot lies in giving up. The maximum certain way updated succeed is usually up-to-date attempt simply one more time"

GDPR, a way to Get Your website equipped

in terms of GDPR and an ordinary weblog those are the principal areas to bear in mind:

person registrations,

remarks,

touch form entries,

analytics,

traffic logs,

safety equipment and plugins.

#1 GDPR and Getting Permission!

personal facts are once in a while called the new Oil or the brand new Gold.

simply ask FB!

till lately many FB users felt they had been the purchaser – but they are no longer.

Advertisers are FB's customers. [Users are the product]

The news approximately facebook and Cambridge Analytica plus different information breaches are converting the way people experience approximately their private facts.

these days' new subscribers want to sense their personal information will be safe with you.

not only that – but that we are able to appreciate the 'permission' they gave us to email them.

by permission – we mean that we are able to handiest email them according to with the authority they gave us when they subscribed.

in case your subscriber requested a loose document or video – that is all they get unless, in addition, they agreed earlier to get hold of more broader communications. (for example, promotions)

So often in the beyond bloggers and statistics entrepreneurs (which include yours actually) have marketed a Lead Magnet but now not explained that going ahead you will also get similarly emails and offers.

Step #3: GDPR is putting an end to that!

We, ourselves are including textbox's to all opt-in paperwork – just like what you notice in the instance under – from our pal and Small commercial enterprise attorney Suzanne Dibble.

GDPR checklist

I'm not a huge fan at the word consent and would advise a few better advertising talk, however it cannot be denied – the goal in Suzanne's choose-in in clean!

in addition, there may be a link to the privateness policy.

observe: The Tick container isn't always pre-ticked.

The GDPR in particular bans pre-ticked decide-in bins.

It calls for granular consent for distinct processing operations.

if you also use SMS or Mail you may want separate TICK bins for each technique of contact.

you furthermore may need to tell subscribers approximately their right to withdraw and provide them smooth ways to withdraw consent (unsubscribe) at any time.

no longer simplest that, individuals have the proper to erasure – also called right to be forgotten

I imagine (however now not positive) that in Suzanne's instance, a subscriber might be sub-divided into people who will acquire each free felony resources (blog posts and so on) and promotions and those that receive free prison resources best – as they did no longer deliver consent to promotions.

For every other example of Tick boxes decide-in checkout this Popup* from PopUp Domination

* presently in Beta trying out and to be had to PopUp Domination customers rapidly.

GDPR multiple tick boxes

Lead Magnets After 25th might also 2018

have you ever signed up for an unfastened record and then been bombarded with a chain of unrelated emails or offers?

Or have we been responsible of doing this ourselves, with our subscribers?

For some of you GDPR will experience like bad information – however I want you to take a look at it in a different way.

Transparency is the important thing...

Do you surely experience emailing a subscriber about something they did now not 'sign on' to is an ideal business?

if your decide-ins and forms are clear and obvious about their purpose you will perhaps get a few fewer subscribers but my prediction is that those who do subscribe may be much more likely to do commercial enterprise with you.

Too many bloggers boast about their variety of subscribers whilst what actually matters is the number of active subscribers who clearly open your email and study them!

deliver me ten thousand energetic fascinated subscribers wherein 25% or more open every email over say 50000 subscribers in which handiest 2% open my email!

Our pals at Aweber these days did a weblog publish on GDPR – it's miles well well worth a examine, mainly in case you are an Aweber patron.

#2 GDPR – The scary felony Stuff!

We do n't need to unduly scare our readers.

but it is important to completely recognize the results of having GDPR wrong.

the European standard facts safety regulation (GDPR) is the most vital change in records privacy law in two decades

the EU well-known records safety law (GDPR) replaces the records protection Directive 95/forty six/EC and was designed to harmonize records privacy legal guidelines across Europe, to shield and empower all EU residents information privacy and to reshape the manner businesses throughout the location approach statistics privateness.

GDPR – Key modifications are designated here

in particular note this remark reference consequences for GDPR non-compliance:

under GDPR agencies in breach of GDPR may be fined up to 4% of annual international turnover or €20 Million (whichever is more). this is the most high-quality that may be imposed for the most extreme infringements e.g.no longer having sufficient consumer consent to manner facts or violating the middle of privateness by means of design concepts. there is a tiered technique to fines e.g. a company may be fined 2% for no longer having their facts in order (article 28), now not notifying the supervising authority and statistics concern approximately a breach or no longer undertaking effect evaluation. it's far essential to notice that those regulations follow to both controllers and processors — meaning 'clouds' will not be exempt from GDPR enforcement.

Step #4: Powers like that get my attention!

The above stated – the general consensus appears to be that until you're real rogue commercial enterprise, the GDPR Compliance Police simply don't have the assets to put in force each mistake or errors simply yet. the principal factor is that we need to be capable of the exhibit we're following best exercise and quick and correctly making it clean for subscribers to unsubscribe/manage their non-public records.

As much as whatever at this degree, the regulatory method appears to be that specialize in schooling and schooling as it is on the investigation.

agencies that demonstrate respect for patron records are in all likelihood to gain large rewards.

in any case, we need to be shielding customers personal information no longer just because the regulation calls for us to – however also because it's the proper thing to do.

if you live in the UK you need to check in with The records Commissioner's office (ICO).

someplace else inside the ecu you need to register along with your neighborhood equivalent.

#3 Your privacy and Cookie policy

when you have not finished already, placed a GDPR cookie coverage in your internet site footer – GDPR has accelerated personal records to include Cookies (while cookies can become aware of an individual it's miles private information)

Likewise with a privacy policy.

luckily there are lots of sources online that permit us to construct our very own privacy and Cookie policies, inclusive of free alternatives.

but I might inspire you to bear in mind a paid for professional service while creating privateness and Cookie regulations.

from time to time unfastened is simply too steeply-priced – in particular when it comes to legal offerings!

Suzanne Dibble (already stated) offers an amazing GDPR package for a cheaper rate, that not handiest covers privateness and Cookies however 18 similarly criminal Template documents & Checklists and Video guides.

Get Suzanne's GDPR bundle here

(I individually control a big number of websites – and this is easily the fine value for cash felony documentation I've ever offered!)

Plugins To manipulate Cookies

Your website may also already have a Cookie Notification that pops up asking for users to agree, but almost honestly in an effort to also need updating to conform to GDPR.

A popular solution is: Cookiebot

Please don't keep in mind this an advice (i have heard each good and terrible approximately Cookiebot) – but up to now, Cookiebot is one of the few plugins that can help you do some of the versions at the Cookie show be aware.

In the instance under – users are most effective devoted to accepting essential Cookies.

This user has already un-ticked advertising cookies, but in the event that they desire, the user could also un-tick possibilities and facts.

cookies, GDPR ecu

this is the last in giving the internet site person control...

however, CookieBot additionally allows you to edit the cookie notice in order that the person has to accept all cookies. [see below]

(or depart web site)

GDPR blogger permit all cookies.

=> Cookiebot allows customers to click on "display details" and spot a display of all the extraordinary cookies getting used at the website.

=> Cookiebot is unfastened for websites of less than a hundred pages. (This consists of class pages, tag pages, web site map and so forth – so attaining one hundred pages for your internet site may be easier than you suspect)

extra resources: (That IncomeDiary has used and advise)

=> Cookie policy

=> GDPR equipped privateness policy

each of the above services additionally provides unfastened alternatives.

WordPress guide For GDPR

it's far understood that WordPress is planning to include GDPR guide in center launch four.nine.6.

This consists of privacy coverage technology from plugin provided facts & additionally anonymizing comments. the launch could be as early as may 2018.

#4 Get existing Subscribers to Re-affirm their Subscription

In most times your subscribers will want to reconfirm their subscription – until you're one of those bloggers who has been very diligent in your signal-up method and may display that your systems at the time your subscriber joined changed into GDPR Compliant.

this is upsetting records marketers.

I want you to take a look at it in another way.

how many in your list honestly care approximately your message – open your emails?

If most effective a small percentage of subscribers are establishing your emails, I'm able to position it to you, that your list in truth, is an awful lot smaller than you suspect.

The time has come for re-engagement and honesty.

If every e-mail you ship out is promoting something and you aren't offering the real fee, then your days as an information Marketer are numbered.

begin an electronic mail re-engagement campaign

move again to your roots and deliver more of that compelling information that your subscribers signed up for inside the first place.

perhaps your Lead Magnet is a touch dated – re-do it and ship it on your list (an advantage free gift with no purpose take delivery of to thank your subscriber for being a subscriber!)

Or do a Survey – discover why human beings subscribed within the first vicinity?

What do they prefer best about your emails? What do they prefer least?

when you have any connection at all, a few humans will respond, supplying you with treasured info to help you cope with their want and write extra enticing content material.

Even ask – why are you now not beginning my emails? (Use that as a subject line on your un-opens)

you may be surprised on the solutions

And don't be afraid to have your subscribers unsubscribe if your message or cloth is now not relevant for them. (Don't take it private)

sometimes bloggers inform me they may be scared of emailing too frequently – and that is possible, but perhaps an excellent larger chance, if you don't e-mail frequently enough.

i am told that the majority on average get 88 emails per day (32,120 in step with yr) – so think about it this manner, in case you simplest electronic mail as soon as a month (12 times) how can you with that 'competition' wish to preserve the relationship and connection going?

humans really do neglect they subscribed!

GDPR is appearing as an aa003e33992aa1e42449a037e2560bf2 for bloggers and the way they build relationships with their list.

That has got to be proper!

bear in mind the 3 E's – educate, Entertain and have interaction.

in the end – and earlier than 25th can also 2018 – e-mail your listing asking them to reconfirm their desire to receive an email from you?

deliver a few severe ideas to the message you wish to convey.

explain the blessings your subscriber gets as a subscriber!

I've heard varying evaluations on the following inspiration and it calls for a diploma of programming expertise – however on the subject of that re-affirmation, give your subscriber alternatives:

a) verify – yes Please, keep sending me emails on [detail service or benefit]

b) No thanks – please unsubscribe me.

In other phrases, a nice sure or a tremendous NO.

seemingly with this option, more people are in all likelihood to choose sure – however, of the route, you have got to get users to open your email within the first vicinity.

To be clear, if your subscriber does now not reply, you'll want to cast off that subscriber from your listing.

This isn't always a genuine example, but look how Sainsbury's use this method while requesting touch permission.

GDPR sure or no options

any other instance...

here's a first-rate example of both the 'live-linked' e-mail and the re-affirm shape from BMW.

word how they detail the benefits of re-confirming! high-quality nonetheless, I did now not want to re-input my e-mail because their tracking gadget knows it is me at my email cope with, re-confirming.

perhaps this will come up with some inspiration.

GDPR re-verify

#5 personal records, sensitive information, and explicit Consent

even though maximum bloggers and records entrepreneurs will now not be dealing with touchy non-public facts it's far critical to be aware the variations and extra IMPORTANTLY whilst specific consent in preference to unambiguous (implied) consent ought to be acquired.

touchy facts

With sensitive information, you ought to always achieve explicit consent from the person.

express consent requires a very clean and unique assertion of consent.

explicit consent has to be obtained via an announcement that has to: "specify the nature of the information that's being accrued, the info of the automatic selection and its effects, or the information of the facts to be transferred and the risks of the switch". (Directive ninety-five/ forty-six/EC, Article 29).

in reality stated: the facts concern have to pretty actually and explicitly say "I consent" for consent to be considered explicit.

There is a superb trendy article on Consent here – along with checklists:

sensitive facts are any information that exhibits:

- Racial or ethnic beginning
- Political evaluations
- nonsecular or philosophical ideas
- alternate union membership
- Genetic facts
- Biometric records for the motive of uniquely identifying a natural man or woman
- records concerning fitness or a natural person's sex existence and/or sexual orientation

For personal facts that aren't always considered touchy – explicit consent isn't always required – as a substitute unambiguous (implied) consent can be enough.

advocated studying: express vs. unambiguous consent: What's the distinction?

example of Unambiguous Consent:

GDPR specific and unambiguous consent

non-public facts are something that incorporates:

- without delay figuring out information together with a person's name, surname, smartphone numbers, and so on.

- Pseudonymous statistics or non-without delay identifying statistics, which does not allow the direct identity of users, however, let in the singling out of individual behaviors (for instance to serve the proper advert to the right consumer on the right second).

=> Consent needs to be given by way of a clean affirmative act – this will include ticking a field while traveling an internet website.

=> Silence, pre-ticked boxes or inactivity does not constitute consent. (Clicking a publish button isn't recognition of phrases)

=> while the processing has more than one purposes, consent has to take delivery of for all of them. (more than one Tick boxes!)

#6 Google Analytics and GDPR

As bloggers and records marketers we adore measuring – site visitors, value Of Sale, Conversions and so forth.

In a thrilling move by way of Google – they have delivered granular records retention controls with Google Analytics.

GDPR and Bloggers

GDPR – frequently asked Questions

At our sister website PopupDomination – we receive a number of questions on GDPR and the consequences for opt-in forms and pop-ups.

unfortunately, there is a lot of inaccurate records and confusion.

In these FAQ's we cope with some of the maximum common questions...

a) With GDPR, do subscribers have to DOUBLE opt-IN a good way to be part of my listing?

the quick solution is not any.

however, as with many stuff – it relies upon.

If for example, you have a Tick container that users should actively tick for you to subscribe and the outcomes of subscribing are flawlessly clear (i.e you have got defined in detail what the user can count on) then a Double opt-in isn't always actually necessary.

further, your structures/records management must be able to reveal what the person without a doubt signed up for, must there ever be a criticism.

b) Do my touch bureaucracy / Quote forms have to be GDPR compliant? (i am an internet-designer)

most net-bureaucracy and primary touch bureaucracy are processed below a legitimate interests basis and consequently, no express consent is required. [Unless you intend to use the data for anything other than what the user may expect]

Quote Requests may be taken into consideration contractual.

c) Is there a limit on how often I can electronic mail my subscribers?

there may be no limit on how often you may e-mail (however you ought to encompass a decide OUT / UN-SUBSCRIBE)

d) I recognize I need to have my subscribers, re-affirm their subscription, however, what if my subscribers do no longer respond or open my e-mail?

With respect – if so, you are higher losing that subscriber out of your list. If like IncomeDiary you are spending large sums on listing control every month, then at the very least, you may be saving some cash!

in the event that they do no longer reply, you may need to cast off that subscriber out of your list.

The simplest exception can be subscribers who live outside the EU – supplied you can become aware of them!

e) My American Processor of data tells me they may be a part of privateness guard and this makes them complain about GDPR. Is it is safe for them to process my facts?

any other quick answer – yes

the European-U.S. and Swiss-U.S. privateness guard Frameworks have been designed with the aid of the U.S. branch of commerce and the EU commission and Swiss management to offer organizations on both sides of the Atlantic with a mechanism to conform with records protection necessities while transferring non-public records from the ecu Union and Switzerland to the use in assist of transatlantic commerce. you may find out greater about privateness defend here

you may check in case your US supplier is certified right here.

f) Do I want a GDPR compliant facts processing settlement? (DPA)

this is a large problem and we aren't going into detail here – plus on many occasions, the larger suppliers and handlers of your records (Aweber, Google and so forth) could have already blanketed this in their agreements/phrases of the provider.

but with smaller providers (for instance your bookkeeper) you could need to have a DPA in place.

there is an amazing article at the DPA here:

In brief...

in which a statistics processor contains out any processing on behalf of a data controller, the statistics controller does no longer follow the DPA except there's a written settlement among the 2 events that includes, at the least, the following clauses:

#1. increase income via including Upsells to present day products

most respectable online entrepreneurs make as a great deal money at the back end as they do on the front cease.

with the aid of what I mean, if they promote a $ ninety-seven product, while a purchaser goes through the checkout manner, they spend at the least another $97 on different products before they complete their purchase.

after I first heard approximately this, I concept it turned into an unbelievable statistic. simply you can't increase income by a hundred% by way of doing something so easy.

We couldn't forget about something that sounded so promising.

the first upsell we ever created become for PopUp Domination. clients would purchase our software, then for the duration of the checkout manner, get provided buying options for multi-website licenses and extra popup designs. fairly, the overnight time we had been capable of growing sales through 2x!

It makes ideal sense. The consumer is already in purchase-mode, they have already got their credit score card out and geared up to shop for something. It's impulse. They see something else they prefer that's related and all they have to do is click one greater button.

Our precise buddy Yanik Silver had a rule of thumb I like to cite:

"60% of humans have to take your first upsell if it's far priced at 60% of the front-give up product rate."

that might be an awesome region to start for most people.

So for instance; in case your front cease product sells at $49, an upsell priced at $27 should convert well.

The only hassle we've got ever had with developing upsells is the technical aspect of factors. the primary time we did it, we had to ask clients to re-enter their credit card information for every upsell they desired to buy.

the absolute confidence this had a negative impact on conversion. despite the fact that we were nevertheless capable of reap that industry general of creating just as plenty from our upsells as the front cease offer.

We aren't tech guys and even asking a programmer to set something up like this will be an ache because it's just no longer something humans have a great deal revel in with.

but things have moved along quite lots due to the fact that we first performed with putting in place upsells.

Our modern-day checkout software SamCart lets in you to create upsells in seconds. All you have to do is insert the income video code, set the fee and it's performed.

clients go from purchasing a product, to upsell page 1, upsell page 2 and ultimately the download web page.

right here's how we set up our upsells:

click on upsells at the left-hand side of your SamCart dashboard after which pick funnels from the drop-down menu.

click "new funnel", upload your funnel name and a quick description, then click "create funnel".

select what number of upsell offers you'd like to feature out of your product listing after which select "enabled." You'll have the choice to feature up to five upsells and five downsells.

Step #5: Adding a Personal Touch to Your Brand Through Influencer Marketing

Word-of-mouth is one of the most valuable forms of marketing as it has been shown to influence 20-50% of all purchasing decisions. People will take the recommendation of a person they know and trust over a corporate ad any day.

Moving beyond family and friends, influencer marketing has weaved its way into a highly sought out form of personal recommendation. To demonstrate this, 40% of Twitter users made a direct purchase because of an influencer's tweet.

Influencer marketing is word-of-mouth for the digital age. Your company can use people with massive online followings to advertise your products on social media. Here's a breakdown of influencer marketing and where to start.

What's an influencer?

A social media influence is someone who leads in a specific niche and can use their following to market products of companies who share the same customer profile as their followers.

There are different types of influencers and more than one might work for your company. Understanding how these types of influencers attract a certain type of customer will help you choose which one is best for your brand.

- Celebrities
- Bloggers
- Micro-influencers

Celebrities are the most popular choice when it comes to endorsements. Major celebrities promote different products that are gifted to them or things they truly love or Instagram or Twitter. Some celebrities eventually go on to become official partners of a brand to create limited edition products and collections.

Influencers don't always have to have a big name. Bloggers are a good choice for an influencer because depending on their field, they may have established a level of authority and expertise. Bloggers with strong followings in health, fashion, or technology have potential to spike an increase in sales with just one promotional post.

Micro-influencers have become extremely popular over Instagram. These people aren't necessarily famous; they just happen to have many followers interested in a specific topic or product to make them a potential partner for a brand.

You may have seen micro-influencers with followers in the hundred-thousand's promoting herbal fit teas, nutritional supplements, or clothing brands.

How do I find an influencer?

A large social media can be compelling enough to sign someone as an influencer for your brand. Don't be so quick to send them your products just yet.

Ask yourself the following questions when considering a potential social media influencer:

- Who are you trying to influence?
- Who do your target customers trust?

An ideal influencer for your brand will need to be relevant to your brand. Remember that they will be sharing your company's content and developing a following based on the market you want to target.

Resonance amongst your audience is another important quality for your influencer to possess. The potential level of engagement that a person can create with your target audience is incredibly valuable to your brand.

The benefits of influencer marketing

With the right influencer, you can reach a very specific audience that is ideal for the product you're selling. By finding an influencer who shares the same interests as your product, you can assume their followers are the same.

A good influencer will be selective in what they choose to promote by rejecting those products they feel their audiences won't gravitate towards.

Influencers want to get something out of your partnership. By creating content that is relatable, engaging, and sharable, influencers are gaining just as much exposure as your product.

With this motivation, the potential to go viral in comparison to a paid ad is much more likely. Organic buzz from these instances is a great way to increase your follower count and build up your email and targeting lists.

Even when a social media post is clearly marked as sponsored content, an influencer provides authenticity to your brand. An influencer that makes your product relatable by weaving their own story into it will receive a genuine response from followers.

70% of consumer's value online opinions even if they don't know the person. Influencers offer a tangible, human aspect to your brand that people can connect with.

Influencer marketing is only increasing in market share. While there are many benefits to incorporating influencers into your marketing strategy, take care to choose a person who embodies your brand and can reach your ideal audience.

Step #6: A Halt in Traffic: Lack of Reviews is Effecting Your Business and Here's Why

Reviews are a great way for your customers to get an idea of what your customer service is like. Through reviews they know what services your offer, how well you offer them, and the quality of your products without even leaving their home.

Reviews are also a valuable tool for a business to know what their customers think about them. It's a convenient way to get honest feedback of your services and find out what you need to fix to keep your customers satisfied.

What your customers say about you is just as much advertising for your business as any marketing strategy you could employ. It's unfiltered, honest, and sometimes a bit dramatic.

While reviews can be loud and sometimes deceiving, no reviews at all can garner the same effect. Are no reviews better than bad reviews? Read ahead to find out.

Is your business good or bad? No one knows...
90% of consumers read online reviews before visiting a business. If there are no reviews, there's no way for a potential consumer to know whether your business is worth visiting or not.

Google has made it convenient to avoid businesses that have a bad reputation without setting foot near their actual establishment. Ensuring good customer service, professionalism, and reliability are now easier than ever.

While this has made the shopping process easier on the consumer, the same can't be said for businesses. Why would a customer visit a business with no online reviews when they can find a place that people can confirm they will have a good experience?

Place yourself in the mindset of a consumer. When you're looking for a product or service, chances are you are not in the mood to experiment with quality and service. A business with a lack of reviews leaves much to the imagination.

Unfortunately, reviews are one of those things that without them, people will stay away. How do you get more reviews to establish the authenticity and reliability that you know your business has?

- Encourage customers who buy a product to review your business at the check-out counter or shopping cart
- Follow-up with a customer to see how they like their product or service and ask permission to publish their responses or quotes

Customers can't trust your business
As with anything, rather than jump into something they know nothing about, customers like to do a little research about a business before they visit. They want to know all about who you are, what you do, and how you do it.

It's fair to say you wouldn't hand your money over to a stranger. Neither would a potential customer trust a business they know nothing about.

For instance, if you're looking to get your wedding cake made, an online review of a local bakery could go a long way. What does this bakery offer? What do their cakes taste like? Are the bakers experienced in making what I want? Will they deliver on time?

You're not going to go to a bakery that has no reviews. What if you get stuck with a cake that looks terrible or tastes… not like cake?

Your customer is the same. 72% of customers say that positive reviews make them trust a local business more an 88% of customers trust online reviews as much as personal recommendations.

Don't make the review process a chore
It's common for people to think "I had a good experience with this company. I don't feel compelled to write a positive review because if my experience wasn't positive, then I would let people know about it".

This mentality follows the idea that people are more likely to post negative reviews rather than positive ones. You need to encourage your customers to move away from this mentality and share their good experiences, just as they share the bad.

Just because there are no positive reviews doesn't mean there are no positive experiences—but your customers don't know that. Increase the amount of positive reviews for your company by making the review process as easy and attractive as possible:

- Send a direct link to your profile on review sites
- Encourage your customer to rate your company on Facebook
- Provide incentive for posting a review
- Create a memorable customer service experience worth sharing

A few reviews are better than no reviews. Make it a point to share your positive reviews across social media platforms for maximum visibility.

The importance of online reviews
Business that are "comfortable" with their following and can't complain about their profits tend to ignore online reviews. They are satisfied with what they can see in front of them, but they have no idea how the internet could ruin their reputation or stunt them from growth.

Online reviews influence:

- Buying decisions
- Online rankings
- Conversion rates

Customers are likely to spend 31% more on a business with "excellent" reviews. Businesses that neglect the importance of online reviews are missing out on profits. They're not necessarily losing money but they could be making a lot more.

There will always be competitors. Online reviews affect how you fare against local competition and can keep you aware of your shortcomings.

The more honest reviews you have, the more your product will sell because customers must find out for themselves if what is being said is true. These reviews are sincere and show that your company has nothing to hide.

Step #7: Why Your Mailing List Is Your Most Powerful Online Marketing Tool

The number one way to really convert website visitors into actual customers is through email correspondence. I can't tell you how many times this has personally worked on me. A company sends an alluring email, you open it, and then realize that hey, this is really cool and the next thing you know, you're about to check out your cart.

This is the real power of email marketing, which many online business owners might underestimate as a powerful lead generating and conversion force. The idea of being an online business does not negate the need to connect with individuals, and emails provide a convenient and also effecitve way to accomplish that. This means that if nothing else, when visitors come to your site, this is the one piece of information you want to ask them to leave with you before they go.

A large following on twitter or Facebook and other social media platforms will never guarantee you the levels of conversion and profitable traffic that email will. In fact, if you get on to platforms like LinkedIn, which has millions of business contacts and prospects, you can get information which will springboard you into making connections and grow your business to proportions you never thought possible.

Step #8: The Benefits of Email Marketing

1. Email marketing provides you with a direct and safe way to interact with customers, and present the offerings of your business to them. The awesome thing is that you get to control the frequency of your emails and also personalize them for your audience.
2. Research has shown that return on investment rates produced as a result of email interactions, are the greatest you will ever receive, than from any other marketing method you use. This means that your company really needs to go all out in terms of collecting email information from prospective clients, and on members in your target groups to really get in on this cash cow.
3. In additon to desktop users, you can reach a wider number of prospects who view emails on their mobile devices. This further increases your scope to make connections, which means that your business will have to consider formatting these emails to be displayed attractively on smaller mobile screens, not just desktops. Don't run the risk of having your valuable messages deleted because they don't display well on a mobile screen, so cover all the bases, and don't let this be a cause for loss of revenue.
4. All you need is an interest catching subject line to encourage your reader's further interest i n exploring the message. You may also chose not to make your message too lengthy. Keeping it simple may be very appealing especially to busy people and also appear more personal.
5. You can easily combine the your email marketing efforts with social media marketing, by using videos for example, in the body of your email, which can

then easily be shared on social media platforms to greatly increase the scope of your reach.

How To Get Your Hands On Mailing Lists

You can acquire email subscriber lists through the database that you have created on your own website. Additonally, you can reach out to mailing list brokers who will provide you with targeted lists, based on your specifications, for a fee. Alternatively, you can get this information through public records,although it may not be as profitable for you as your own company list or a puchased targeted listing.

Step #9:Why You Need To Get Into The Mind Of Your Audience

If you're looking to drive sales through increased traffic to your website and grow your business, the key determinants of this are your site visitors, your audience. The only way to truly see your marketing efforts pay off is to identify the clients most likely to engage your business, and produce a conversion for your product or service. To get hold of this information, there are a lot of software and programs available to help you collect this valuable data.

Many entrepreneurs spend generously on marketing campaigns to yield good conversion rates for their businesses. Garnering information based on the habits of your potential clients is a solid way to determine if many of your strategies are viable. Using software that can both gather and analyze your data will save you much time, instead of having to do it manually, and will provide you with well needed direction for the implementation of future strategies.

Once you have the data in hand, it's time to get to work. These programs will provide you with basic information such as gender, age, and location. While these are good metrics to have, they really don't tell you much, so a more sophisticated program which gives more substantial information relating to their educational background, their social media and general internet habits, and even where they live, gives a more complete picture of your ideal client-the one who will convert for you.

Since audience reach is a big deal, it's likely that your marketing budget may be quite sizeable. The results of your audience information search will help you to see if you need to pump money into other areas of marketing or if the methods you're currently using will suffice, or can be utilized in more effective ways.

The money you've spent on marketing and advertising is an investment in your business, for which you'd like to see returns. This targeted information will help you to figure out when and where your most likely clients shop and browse, then, you can use directed advertising to appeal to them on those platforms. When you're clear about your brand and what you want it to say to potential clients, leveraging this along with the information you were previously armed with, will help you reach them in a most effective way and will yield the conversion you seek for your business.

It's more than likely that you conduct business online as well and have seen pop up ads and other forms of advertising which make you wonder how these sites are able to determine your interests. This is because many of these sites use the same strategies with you, that you'd like to use with your clients, to increase your own profitability. It must be very clear now how this approach makes a lot of sense.

There's no miraculous way to generate greater website traffic which converts to sales. Using structured and proven approaches which generate meaningful information, like this one, really is a logical way of gauging how to position yourself from a marketing perspective, thus putting you in a prime position to engage with your target audience.

Naturally, you'd love greater insight as to where you can get a hold of a host of internet marketing tips and strategies to increase your conversion rate and grow your business..

Step #10: How To Use Targeted Ads To Generate Traffic With Facebook

With the billions of people who use Facebook all over the world, this platform represents a gold mine when it comes to reaching people and generating traffic for your online business. As an entrepreneur you always have to be thinking about the most effective ways to raise the profitability of your business and this seems to be one of the obvious choices.

We're not just talking about free advertising. Using the free method gives you a much smaller scope of reach than paid advertising would with Facebook. You can choose the frequency and the scope of your campaign, and also determine how to position if your business offering fits in with their advertising models.

How To Do It?
You have the option of promoting your business through posts made on your page, directing users to your website, and Facebook page promotion. What will prove most effective for you, is to have users directed to your website, which shifts the focus from your Facebook page and have prospects looking where the real action takes place. This is what will increase your chances of making an actual sale.

Through Facebook's platform you'd already have made choices as to the demographic you're interested in reaching so each visitor is a potential client. You're already attracting the kind of traffic you're looking for.

Develop The Art
You need to bear in mind that Facebook users in most cases are looking to connect with people they know or are seeking out acquaintances. Their primary focus tends not to be on making a purchase. You will find though that pages offering a service tend to do pretty well. You'll therefore need to consider how to create a catchy ad, which will capture your audience's attention and urge them to consider giving you more than passing glance.

The ideal approach is not to try to fill an already existing need; ads are full of this. You want to create a demand, which is more likely to get you noticed and followed. Of course the objective is always to move the traffic to your website.

How To Properly Target?

Facebook offers you so many choices in terms of deciding which categories of individuals you want your ads to target. Among the most important categories are location, gender, age and interests.

You really want to zoom in on the matter of the interest of your audience and we're not just talking about their general interests only. While this may be somewhat helpful in determining what might be appealing to them, the real winner is the specific interests they've listed on their profile.

In looking at their specific interests, you also want to take it a step further by researching just how much those interests mean to them. This will allow you to really fine tune your target audience so that your likelihood of traffic generation and ultimately conversion, will increase.

Ad Structure
You also want to give attention to the structure of your ads in order to target properly. You can use original, purchased or (legally) free images to promote your ad. Choose carefully so that your image will speak to or resonate with your targeted audience.

Use clear and concise text with an easy to read and understand message. This is where you'll have to find your creative side, or draw on the expertise of someone, paid or otherwise, who can assist you with wording.

If you have a business model that will allow you to make effective use of Facebook's advertising platform, then learning how to utilize it effectively will help you create targeted ads for the right demographic. Making use of the tips provided and taking the time to get familiar with the ins and outs of the advertising platform, will generate traffic and revenue for your online business.

www.ingramcontent.com/pod-product-compliance
Lightning Source LLC
Chambersburg PA
CBHW041949240526
45473CB00036B/2850